CHINESE CHARACTER STORIES

CHINESE CHARACTER STORIES

Expanded 2nd Edition

by

Wen-Juan Fu

First published 2017

Revised 2nd edition © 2020

by Wen-Juan Fu

ISBN : 979-8-6319-7456-2

For free videos and other learning resources visit

chinesecharacterstories.wordpress.com

Contents

目录 *mù lù*

Introduction by Joseph Cornejo

This book serves to introduce the reader to the Chinese written language. As a native English speaker who has lived in China for several years, I know very well how confusing Chinese can be for those of us who are unfamiliar with it. Whereas Spanish or German or French will have a certain familiarity to English speakers because of the Greek and Latin roots of many common words, Chinese seems utterly foreign. The spoken language is tonal, so that the same word — or rather, what we think of as the same word — can have totally different meanings depending on how it is said. (As an example, "ma" can mean "mother" or "horse" depending on the tone. Remember that next time you're talking to your mom!) And if that

3

wasn't enough, the written language isn't based on letters that represent sounds, but on pictures that represent things and ideas.

Most books and teaching systems rely on simple memorization of the characters, their sounds, and their meanings. And for this reason, the study of Chinese is off-putting to many people. Whereas an English learner just has to learn twenty-six letters and the rules of phonics to have a basic foundation, a Chinese learner has to learn over one thousand characters just to be at an "elementary" level according to the HSK system for testing Chinese proficiency.

But, as a famous Chinese proverb says, 千里之行，始於足下 *qiān lǐ zhī xíng, shǐ yú zú xià* — "A journey of a thousand miles begins with a single step." This book is designed to be that first step, and to give you a way of thinking about the Chinese written language that not only makes memorization easier, but makes learning the language both more fun and more interesting.

The first key to learning and remembering the Chinese characters is to understand them. To do this requires some knowledge of their cultural and historical context. This doesn't mean that you have to read a bunch of books about China's five thousand years of history in order to understand the language. But if you know and understand some key points from that history and from Chinese culture, the written language will begin to make sense to you as a system, and not just a random assortment of brush strokes.

For this reason, *Chinese Character Stories* contains a lot of information and anecdotes which not only introduce the reader to certain aspects of Chinese culture and tradition, but also serve to illuminate the meanings of words and characters, thereby making it much easier to remember them.

As an example, take the character for "king" or "emperor" — 王 *wáng*. Without context, it has no meaning at all. But, as the author explains in Chapter 7, the three horizontal lines of this character represent what the ancient Chinese called "the three powers" of Heaven, Earth, and Humanity. The vertical line represents the duty and function of the king, which is to unite the three powers into one. Once you know this, you can see the logic in how the character is written, and you also have a mnemonic device for remembering the meaning, which brings us to the second key.

The second key to learning and remembering Chinese characters is to have a mnemonic device to assist your memory.

Each character introduced in this book has an explanation and discussion of its meaning which includes a story, a fun fact, or a visualization based on the shape of the character. We have an easier time remembering things that are interesting or fun. If you associate these stories or images with the characters, you will find yourself remembering them almost without effort.

At the end of each chapter, you will find a worksheet with space for you to practice writing the characters yourself, as well as instructions for how to write the characters from the first stroke to the last. You can practice in the book itself, but it's also recommended that you practice on your own paper.

The third key to learning Chinese characters is the same key to learning anything else: practice, practice, practice!

While we wish we could give you some kind of magic formula for learning written Chinese instantly and effortlessly, like the way Neo learns kung fu in *The Matrix*, the real world isn't like that.

Actually writing the characters yourself — over and over again — is important because it imprints the shapes of the characters into your muscle memory. If you think back to when you were little and first learning English, you might remember that at first, it was rather difficult to write your ABC's, for the simple reason that you'd never done it before. You had to copy the shapes from pictures, and sometimes your writing looked very sloppy. But eventually, with practice, you improved. Now you write in English without even thinking about it. With enough practice, you can write in Chinese the same way.

You'll notice that some other characters are sometimes referenced in the descriptions. If you don't know them yet, don't worry about them. The essential lessons are the characters that are featured and described.

A Note on ancient Chinese Characters:

小篆 *xiǎo zhuàn* calligraphy is a form of Chinese writing that dates from the Qin Dynasty (221 B.C.-206 B.C.). *Qin Shi Huang* 秦始皇 was the founder of the Qin Dynasty. He unified the Seven Warring States and created the first Chinese empire. His minister 李斯 *Lǐ Sī* combined the texts of the seven states to develop a common written language, which is called 小篆 *xiǎo zhuàn* - "small seal." This is one of the earliest forms of written Chinese.

Since the 小篆 *xiǎo zhuàn* characters often look more like pictures of the things that they represent, we often make use of them in this book to see how modern characters evolved from them.

10

Chapter 1

人 rén human beings

This character is 人 *rén*. In ancient times, only slaves were called *rén*, while upper class people were called 君 *jūn*, 臣 *chén*, or 大夫 *dài fū*. So the old version of the *rén* character was a man on his knees with hands touching the ground. But now *rén* is 人, which is a person standing upright. Imagine a man with his arms folded across his chest, standing with his legs apart. I think the change from the old version of the character signifies that all human beings have dignity and value.

大 dà big

The *xiǎo zhuàn* version of 大 *dà* is the 人 *rén* character with his shoulders lifted up, standing up with two legs spread, which aims at showing his power. But the modern character looks like a man with arms outstretched, ready to give you a big hug.

天 tiān heaven

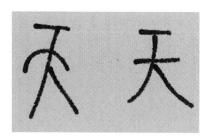

The *xiǎo zhuàn* version of 天 *tiān* is the character 大 *dà* with an additional line on the top. It refers to the things that are above human beings. I like to think of it this way: even a big man is still below heaven.

Now that you have learned these three characters, let's look at the way Chinese characters can change into each other with the addition of extra strokes:

人 *rén* -- 大 *dà* -- 天 *tiān* --
夫 *fū*

夫 fū adult male, as in 丈夫 zhàng fū,

husband

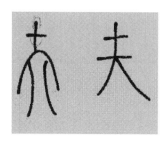

The character 夫 *fū* is a picture of a man who worked as a scholar for the king in ancient times. These men were called 士大夫 *shì dà fū*. Nowadays, 夫 *fū* is usually used to mean a grown up man who is responsible, as in the saying 匹夫有責 *pǐ fū yǒu zé* – "Each man has a duty to his country." 夫 *fū* is also found in the word for "husband," 丈夫 *zhàng fū*.

夫 *fū* is only a little different in appearance from 天 *tiān*. I like to think of it

16

this way: only a man who can hold up the heavens is responsible and able to be a husband. Also, in the old days men had long hair, and so they needed a stick to tie their hair. So 夫 is a big man 大 with a stick in his hair, as in the above illustration. You can also think of it as a man wearing a Fedora-style hat.

Practice.

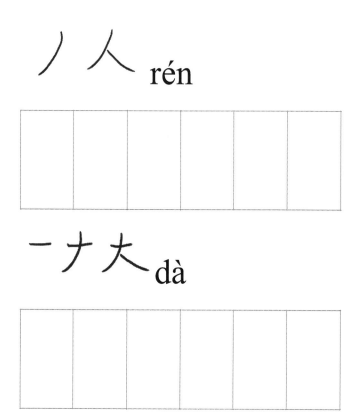

丿 人 rén

一 ナ 大 dà

 tiān

 fū

Chapter 2

十 shí   <small>ten</small>

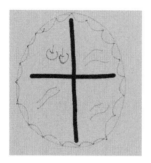

十 *shí* is a cross, but the vertical is longer than the horizontal, just like the Christian symbol. 十 *shí* means "ten." Twenty is 二十 *èr shí*, thirty is 三十 *sān shí*, etc. This character also means "to divide things." Imagine if you put a 十 *shí* into a cake, you would divide the cake into four pieces. 十 *shí* is the skeleton of many Chinese characters. You will learn some of them in this chapter.

干 gān dry,

gàn trunk, do, work, main part

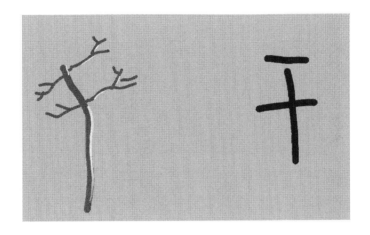

One more horizontal stroke on the top of 十 *shí* makes 干 *gān*. 干 *gān* was a tool for hunting, it was made of wood from tree. Now *gan* pronounced with the forth tone means "tree branch" and also "working." Pronounced with the first tone, it means "dry." I think the basic meaning is tree branch, and all the meanings are connected. Think of it this way: the hunting tool is made of a tree branch; tools are for work; and in order to make a tool from a tree branch, the wood has to be dry. 干 *gān* is very often used in 干杯 *gān bēi*, which means "Cheers." The literal meaning is "dry glass" — in other words, drink every last drop in your cup. However, we sometimes add something like "drink the amount you like" after 干杯 *gān bēi* so that people don't have to get too drunk.

平 píng   flat , even, fair

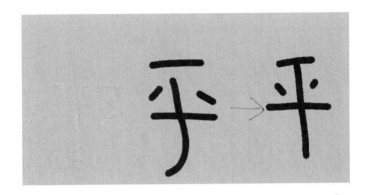

The addition of two small strokes to 干 *gān* makes 平 *píng*. 平 *píng* is usually used as 公平 *gōng píng*, which means "fair." We can think of it this way: if you put one piece of rice on each side of the scales, it will be balanced and fair.

木 mù wood; tree

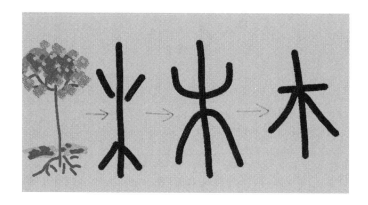

The character 木 *mù* is a picture of a tree. This might not be obvious to Western readers, who are used to picturing a tree with a slim trunk and large branches extending out. In this character, the bottom strokes are the roots, the horizontal stroke is the ground level, and the top is the branches. If you think about it, a tree has deep roots that spread far and wide below the ground, and that is what you see in this character.

Since we know that 十 *shí* is the basis of this character, we can also think of it this way: 木 *mù* is 十 *shí* and 人 *rén* together.

米 mǐ   rice

In the early days, 米 *mǐ* was the character for "wheat." (Nowadays, wheat is 小麦 *xiǎo mài*.) The old character was a picture of wheat growing on branches. Nowadays, 米 *mǐ* means rice. I like to think of 米 *mǐ* this way: two pieces of little rice grow on a tree. Although rice does not really grow on trees, you can think of the two dots as the fruit of the tree, the part that people can eat.

来 lái　　come; arrive

In ancient times, 来 was pronounced as *mài*, and it meant "barley." That is why it is shaped like a plant. Later, the Chinese created the character 麦 *mài* for "barley," so the pronunciation of 来 changed to *lái*. It has one more horizontal stroke than 米 *mǐ*. 米 *mǐ* and 来 *lái* both have 木 *mù* inside, since both originally referred to plants. So, what story we can give to 来 *lái* ? Think of it this way: a tree, 木 *mù*, produces fruit: 米 *mǐ*. When that happens, it is harvest time. The harvest has come, has arrived. The extra horizontal stroke at the top of the character can be thought of as a calendar mark, denoting the arrival of the harvest time or even as a slash from a tool used to cut fruit from the tree. Remember, the most important thing about Chinese character stories is that they are pneumonic devices to help you remember the meaning of the character, so use whatever works best for you!

Practice.

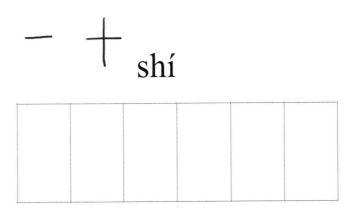

─ 十 shí

─ 二 干 gàn

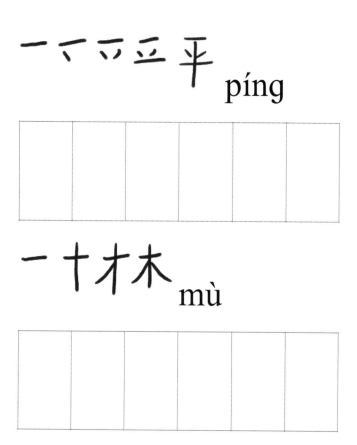

一 丆 丏 五 平 píng

一 十 才 木 mù

丶 丷 丷 半 斗 米 mǐ

一 丷 二 二 丰 来 来 lái

Chapter 3

In last two chapters, we learned 木 *mù,* and 人 *rén.* Now we can have some fun with these characters.

林 lín forest, grove

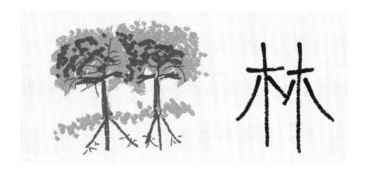

林 *lín* consists of two 木 *mù,* so you can guess the meaning. Multiple trees make a forest or grove. Now you can translate a common English expression into partial Chinese: He can't see the 林 *lín* for the 木 *mù*!

森 sēn forest

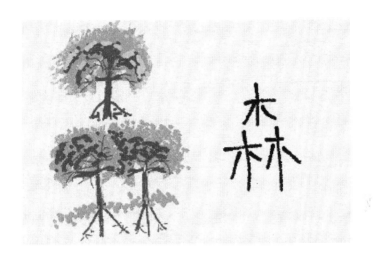

森 *sēn* consists of three 木 *mù*, so you might think it means something more like a jungle or forest — and you are right! Normally, 森 *sēn* is used together with 林 *lín* — 森林 *sēnlín* means "forest."

休 xiū   to have a rest

休 *xiū* consists of 人 *rén* and 木 *mù*. It shows man leaning next to a tree, having a rest. So its meaning is "to stop" or "to have a rest."

从 cóng to follow; come from

从 *cóng* consists of two 人 *rén*. You might think it means a lot of people, but it doesn't. Instead, it depicts a man walking after another man. So its basic meaning is "to follow." Indeed, the first 人 *rén* is following the second so closely, it looks like he's about to step on his heel!

众 zhòng　a lot of people

众 *zhòng* consists of three 人 *rén*. As you probably can guess, it means "many people." In the old days, 众 *zhòng* could mean "lots of people" by itself, such as in the old saying of Mencius: 独乐乐不如众乐乐 *dú yuè lè bù rú zhòng yuè lè*, which means: "The happiness that comes from playing music with other people is more than that from playing alone." Nowadays, 众 *zhòng* is mostly used in compound words with other characters.

Practice.

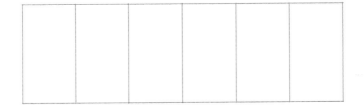

一 十 才 木
木 村 材 林 lín

木   柔
森   sēn

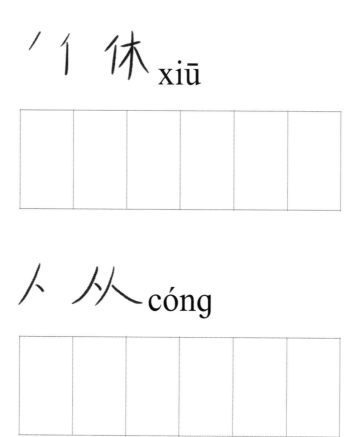

丿亻休 xiū

人 从 cóng

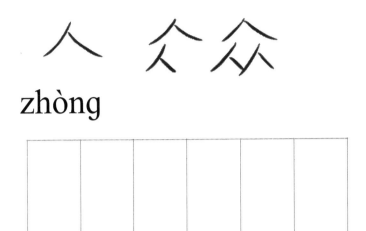

zhòng

Chapter 4

未 wèi have not; did not

未 *wèi* has one more horizontal stroke than 木 *mù*, which is shorter than the one below it. This stroke means a new, fresh branch is going to grow longer in the future. That why we use 未 in the word for "future," 未来 *wèi lái*, which means that which has not come yet.

末 mò tip; ending part

 末 *mò* looks very similar to 未 *wèi* because it also has one more horizontal stroke than 木 *mù*. But this one is longer than the old branch. So, it is at the tip, and means "the ending part."

本 běn origin; foundation

 本 *běn* has a horizontal stroke near the bottom of the tree trunk. The root is the foundation of a tree, so 本 *běn* means "origin" or "foundation."

本 *běn* and 末 *mò* have opposite meanings, and we can see this clearly by the shapes of the characters.

There is an old saying: 本末倒置 *běn mò dǎo zhì*, which means "to confuse the branch and the root," to mistake the unimportant for the important. It is similar to the English phrase, "to put the cart before the horse."

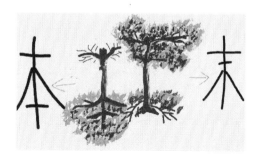

Practice.

 wèi

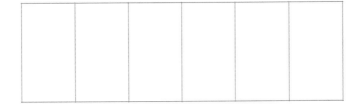

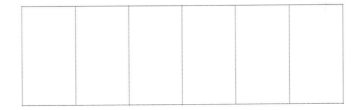 mò

 běn

Chapter 5

水 shǔi <small>water</small>

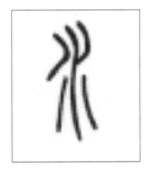 

The ancient character for water is a picture of waves. In the current version, this is not as clear, so I like to think of 水 *shǔi* as water coming out of a faucet, maybe a broken faucet where instead of one big stream, you have several different streams shooting out everywhere!

火 huǒ fire

火 *huǒ* means "fire." The basis of this character is 人 *rén* with two more strokes added to it. There are two ways you can think of 火 *huǒ*: First, a living human body gives off heat – Chinese medicine says that each person has the 命门火 *mìng mén huǒ*, the "life-gate fire," in the deep core of their body. Second, it was humans who learned how to make fire, which changed our species forever. Or, if neither of these stories works for you, maybe you can just think of that Denzel Washington movie, *Man On Fire!*

口 kǒu mouth

 口 *kǒu* is the shape of an open mouth, and that is one of its main meanings. If you see 口 *kǒu* as one of the shapes in a character, next to other shapes, that indicates something related to the mouth. For example, 吐 *tù*, "to spit." If 口 *kǒu* is the largest shape in the character, and has other shapes inside of it, that means that it has something to do with a defined area. For example, 口 *kǒu* is the root of the word for "country," 国 *guó*, because a country is defined by its borders.

If we put 十 (we learned it in chapter 2) into a 囗, 十 will divide the big 囗 (remember, big 囗 means a defined space), what will happen? Try it by yourself and check the answer in the next chapter!

Practice.

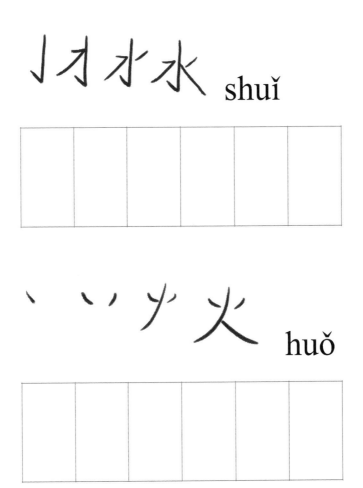

丿 丬 水 水 shuǐ

丶 丶ヽ ⺍ 火 huǒ

丨 冂 口

kǒu

Chapter 6

田 tián field; farmland.

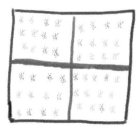

Putting 十 *shí* into 口 *kǒu*, we get 田 *tián*. We know a big 口 *kǒu* means an area - adding 十 *shí* can divide this area into multiple spaces. In ancient times, the first division of land was for agriculture. Even today, crops are planted in rows, which make lines in the soil. You can think of 田 *tián* as a field divided into sections for different crops. Or you can think of it as a large piece of land, divided into pieces for four different farmers.

甲 jiǎ first; shell; nail (fingernail or

toenail)

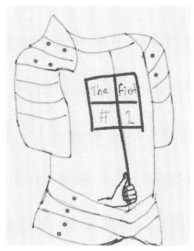

甲 jiǎ was a word for a soldier's armor like in 盔甲kuī jiǎ. Nowadays it is used as nail — 指甲zhǐ jia or first place — 甲等jiǎ děng. It looks similar to 田 *tián*, but the important difference is the longer vertical stroke in the center. To remember the difference, you can think of it this way: the longer down stroke makes it look like a sign that someone might hold at the bottom, or like the mast of a ship.

囚 qiú imprison; prisoner

If we put 人 *rén* into 囗 *kǒu*, it looks like the person has been locked up — and that's exactly what it means! I think this one is pretty easy to understand, as long as you remember that 人 *rén* is a person.

困 kùn to trap, to surround, sleepy

Putting a 木 *mù* into 口 *kǒu*, we get 困 *kùn*. Actually, you might notice that the 木 *mù* character looks a little different in the bottom right corner. A tree can't grow in a dark house, maybe it even gets sick. So 困 *kùn* usually means being trapped in a bad situation. A common phrase is 困难 *kùn nán*, which means "difficulties." 困 *kùn* also means "sleepy." This is because the traditional form of 困 *kùn* was 睏. As we will learn later, 目 *mù* means "eye," so 睏 *kùn* means that the eyes are surrounded, as if a person's heavy eyelids were imprisoning the eyes! People don't use the traditional form that much now, but the meaning of "sleepy" has stayed.

回 huí to circle, to go back, to return

Putting a 口 *kǒu* into a bigger 口 *kǒu*, we get 回 *huí*, which means "to return." The character originally portrayed water going around in a spiral. The original meaning of 回 *huí* is "rotating." It is most often used as part of 回来 *huí lái*, "to come back". To me, it looks like frontal view of a bus, driving through a tunnel, returning home after a long journey. Get out of the way — it's headed right toward you!

品 pǐn taste; quality

品 *pǐn* is formed by three 口 *kǒu*, just like the characters we have already learned, 森 *sēn* and 众 *zhòng*. The basic meaning of 品 *pǐn* is "taste," as in the verb 品尝 *pǐn cháng*, "to taste or sample." It can also mean "quality," as in 品 质 *pǐn zhì*.

To remember this, think of the double meaning of the English word "taste" — it can mean the sense of taste in your mouth, and it can also mean your ability to discern good quality from bad. If someone knows what good quality is, we say that they *have good taste*.

Practice.

tián

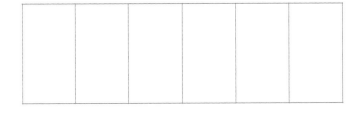

jiǎ

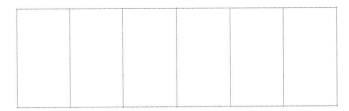

冂 冈 囚 qiú

冂 闲 困 kùn

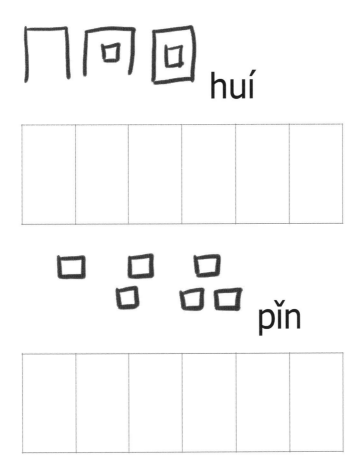

huí

pǐn

<u>Chapter 7</u>

日 **rì** the sun

The character for the sun was originally a dot with a circle around it, symbolizing the sun with a halo of light. Over time, the circle became the 囗 character, and the dot became a horizontal stroke inside of it. Words have 日 *rì* as a part of it all connect with time.

旦 dàn the next day; dawn

旦 *dàn* is formed by a sun and a line. The line stands for the horizon, or the Earth. So when the sun is rising from the horizon, it is another new day.

早 zǎo　early; morning

The character for "morning" is made by adding a vertical stroke to 旦 *dàn*. This extra stroke symbolizes the shadow of a tree being cast by the sunshine in the early morning. Alternatively, you can think of it as a ray of sunshine, emanating from the sun down to the Earth below.

亘 gèn   stretch or extend

We learned that the horizontal 一 *yī* below 日 *rì* is the Earth. The horizontal 一 *yī* above 日 *rì* is heaven. People observed that the sun moves between the Earth and heaven, so they invented 亘 *gèn* to mean things that extend all the way across, from one place or time to another. It is commonly seen in 亘古 *gèn gǔ*, meaning "throughout time" or "since antiquity." There is also the saying, 亘古不变

gèn gǔ *bú biàn*, which means "from time immemorial" and refers to something that is unchanging over time.

古 gǔ ancient; age-old

The second character in 亘古 *gèn gǔ* is the character for "ancient." You can see that it consists of 口 *kǒu* with 十 *shí* on top of it. (Although 十 *shí* by itself is written with a longer vertical stroke, when it is used as part of another character, it often has a longer horizontal stroke, as in 早 *zǎo*, which we learned previously.) So what is it about ten mouths that means "ancient?" I like to look at it this way: in ancient times, there were usually ten people in a family, so there were ten mouths to feed.

王 wáng   emperor, king

In ancient Chinese philosophy, there is the idea of the 三才 *sān cái*, the Three Powers: 天 *tiān*, "heaven," 地 *dì*, "earth," and 人 *rén*, "humanity." The sacred duty of the emperor is to unite heaven and earth, to be the connection between the three powers. So in the character for "emperor," the three horizontal lines (just like 三 *sān*, "three") represent heaven, humanity, and earth, while the vertical line connecting all three represents the Emperor or King. This is one of my favorite Chinese characters because of the way it contains so much information about ancient Chinese culture and philosophy. The Chinese believe that tigers have the character 王 *wáng* on their heads, and therefore they, and not lions, are the real "kings of the jungle."

晶 jīng   shiny, sparkling

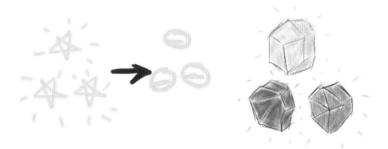

Three 人 *rén* is 众 *zhòng*, three 口 *kǒu* is
品 *pǐn*, three 木 *mù* is 森 *sēn*, so what about
three 日 *rì*? If there were three suns, it would
be incredibly bright and shiny, and that is the
meaning of 晶 *jīng*. In this character, 日 *rì*
actually means "star" and not sun, although of
course the sun is a star. The sparkling of the
stars in the night sky is similar to the way
that crystals reflect light, and so 晶 *jīng* is
commonly used in words for "crystal," such as
水 晶 *shuǐ jīng*. (Review lesson: what does 水
shuǐ mean again?)

Practice.

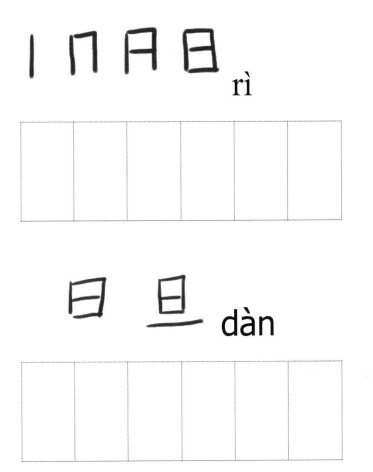

丨 冂 冂 日 rì

日 旦 dàn

旦 旦 早 zǎo

一 百 亘 gèn

 gǔ

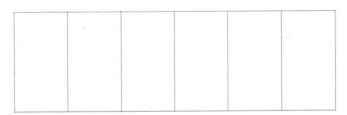

wáng

jīng

Chapter 8

子 zǐ   person; son; seed

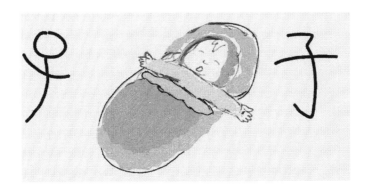

子 zǐ stands for person or son. If you look at the ancient version of the character, you can see that it is the picture of a little baby with its arms reaching out for its mommy. So people use 子 zǐ after their name to show that they are modest. In olden times, it was also a title of respect for very learned people. You might know the names of famous Chinese philosophers like 孔子 kǒng zi

(Confucius) or 老子 lǎo zi. Although 子 zǐ is pronounced with the third tone when it is by itself, it does not have a tone when it follows other words, which is why it doesn't have any tone marks in the above names.

子 zǐ means "seed" as in 种子 zhǒngzi. As we know, seeds are a plant's sons.

子 zǐ is also part of my nickname, 娟子 Juān zi, but I'm not sure if it's because I'm modest or because I'm wise. :)

儿 ér little child

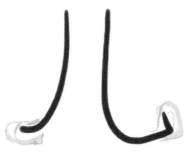

儿 *ér* comes from the picture of a little child playing, and it means "little child." The modern character looks like a child's two little legs, which is a good way to remember it. 儿 *ér* is used to make the words for "son" and "daughter." 儿子 *ér zi* - "son," and 女儿 *nǚ ér* - "daughter." We just learned that 子 *zǐ* means "son," so we can understand 儿子 *ér zi* easy enough. Below, we will learn the other character in 女儿 *nǚ ér*.

75

女 nǚ woman; female

The character in the picture above is 女 *nǚ,* which means "woman." As you can see, the old *xiǎo zhuàn* version is a representation of a woman on her knees. In earlier times, the social status of Chinese women was low, and they were required to kneel down to their parents, brothers, husbands, and their husband's parents. So this kneeling down posture became associated with women.

好 hǎo good

Sometimes two or more characters combine together to form compound words, like 女儿 *nǚ ér*. But other times, two characters actually combine to form one, new character. That is the case here with 好 *hǎo*, which, as you can see, is made up of 女 *nǚ* and 子 *zǐ*. 好 *hǎo* is one of the most common words in Chinese because it means "good." The ancient Chinese symbolized goodness with the image of a mother and son. There are several different ideas about exactly why this was, such as the importance that was placed on male children in earlier times. But I prefer to think that the love between mother and child is one of the greatest goods in human life, and thus the best symbol for the idea of good.

One of the most common uses of 好 *hǎo* is in the word for "hello" - 你好 *nǐ hǎo!*

兄 xiōng older brother; buddy

兄 *xiōng* is made up of 儿 *ér* and 口 *kǒu*, so it's a mouth with legs! This is the character for "elder brother." You might think that it represent how much food a young man eats — but actually, it comes from the old tradition of the eldest son having a position of authority in the family. Since his words were to be obeyed, the mouth in this character actually represents speech, not eating. (Of course, sometimes older brothers have a "big mouth," so maybe that had something to do with it, too.) We usually use 兄长 *xiōng zhǎng* for "older brother" and 兄弟 *xiōng dì* for "brothers" or "buddies."

光 guāng light

光 *guāng* is the character for "light." It is formed by combining the top part of 火 *huǒ* and 儿 *ér* together, with 一 *yī* in the middle, dividing them. So we have one child, and a fire giving off light. Parents often say that their child is the "light of their life," so I like to remember this character in this way.

先 xiān   before; earlier; first

If we look at the ancient *xiǎo zhuàn* form of this character, we know that 先 *xiān* is actually formed by 止 *zhǐ* (see the next character) and 儿 *ér*. 止 *zhǐ* was originally a picture of a foot, and so the original image of 先 *xiān* was a foot on top of a pair of legs! This was meant to symbolize someone who walks in front of others. If he walks in front, he arrives before the others, and so 先 *xiān* now means "before" or "earlier."

81

止 zhǐ to stop

As we learned in the previous section, 止 *zhǐ* was changed from a picture of a foot, and that was its original meaning. When it is used as a part of a character, its shape changes, as you can see with 先 *xiān*. The top part of 先 *xiān* doesn't really look like 止 *zhǐ*, but it is.

Just as the image of 止 *zhǐ* changed from the old days, so did its meaning. Today, it doesn't mean "foot" – we use another character with the same pronunciation, 趾 *zhǐ*, for that. 止 *zhǐ* means "to stop." Fortunately, it's easy to remember this because it looks like two different kinds of walls or fences sticking up from the ground. I like to think of the one on the right as having a basketball hoop sticking out of it. No matter if you're walking from the right or left, you aren't getting through those walls. "Stop!"

Practice.

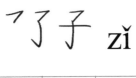 zǐ

 ér

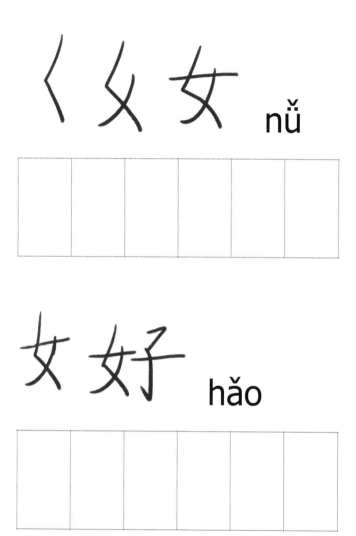

く ㄠ 女 nǚ

女 好 hǎo

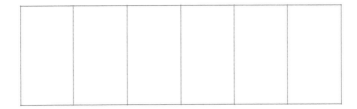

guāng

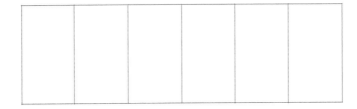

xiān

丨 卜 卟 止

zhǐ

Chapter 9

舌 shé tongue

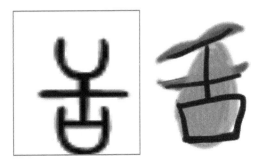

舌 *shé* is the character for "tongue." If you look at the old *xiǎo zhuàn* version, this is more obvious because of the curved shape of the upper and lower portions. Nowadays, 舌 *shé* is made from 古 *gǔ*, which we learned previously, with the addition of a ノ (a left falling stroke called *piě*.) It's important to remember that the uppermost stroke is not horizontal, but actually slants down to the left a little bit. Sometimes, when a person sticks out his or her tongue, it slants to one side, so that is a good way to remember this character – just stick out your tongue and point it down and to the left!

言 yán   speech; word

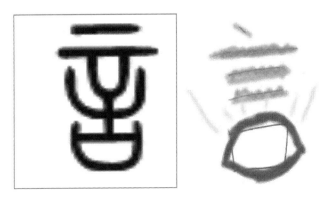

Looking at the old version of 言 *yán* and comparing it with the old version of 舌 *shé,* we can see that two extra lines have been added. These symbolize that something more than just the tongue has come out of the mouth – this person has spoken! Nowadays 言 *yán* is written with 口 *kǒu* and three horizontal lines over it, as well as the small dot on top, which is called *diǎn.* I like to think of these lines as sound waves coming out of a person's mouth as they speak.

舌 *shé* is also a radical for making other characters, although it looks totally different. When it becomes a radical, it changes to 舌 , which I've always thought looks very similar to a lowercase "i."

说 shuō speak; say

说 *shuō* is formed by the radical 讠 and the character 兑 *duì*. You'll notice that 兑 *duì* is just like 兄 *xiōng*, which we learned earlier, but with two extra "dots" on top. By itself, 兑 *duì* means "to exchange," "to convert," or "to add." Why do the two extra "dots" change the meaning from "elder brother" to "convert?" I'm not sure, but I like to think of the two dots as ears. Your older brother hears things in the world and is aware of things that you aren't, and often has to translate or convert this information into something you can understand.

Why does adding the 讠 radical in front of 兑 duì change the meaning to "speak?" Putting the 讠 radical in front of 兑 duì means this is a way of communication that is through talking.

There are a couple different ways to remember the meaning of 说 *shuō*. First, you can remember that the 兑 *duì* character is basically a mouth with legs (and ears), and imagine that he is speaking out of his big, open mouth. But to me, 兑 *duì* looks more like an old television set from back when they all had rabbit ear antennas. So I imagine that someone is on television, and they are speaking, because the 讠 radical lets us know this character is about words.

Practice.

shé

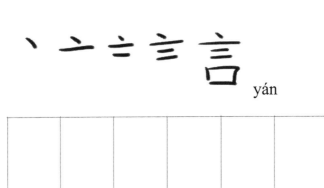

yán

丶 讠 讠 讱 说 说 shuō

Chapter 10

土 tǔ soil; ground

If you remember from Chapter 7, a horizontal line at the bottom of a character often signifies the earth. 土 *tǔ* is the image of a plant springing up from the soil. You can think of it in two ways: The bottom line is the earth, and the 十 *shí* character is a plant growing out of it. Or, you can think of the upper horizontal stroke as the ground, and the lower horizontal stroke as the plant's roots under the earth, similar to 木 *mù* from Chapter 2.

Notice that the next character, 士 *shì*, looks very similar to 土 *tǔ*. The important difference is that in 土 *tǔ*, the bottom horizontal stroke is longer, because the character means "soil," and that is the important element.

士　shì　bachelor (in ancient China); scholar; soldier

士 *shì* looks a lot like 土 *tǔ*, but they are very different in meaning. In the old days, 士 *shì* was a picture of an ax, and it was used in reference to soldiers. It also meant "bachelor," and you can see the connection, because young unmarried men are often conscripted as soldiers.

Nowadays, 士 *shì* is often used in words related to educated people, such as doctors or academics. The shape of the character makes me think of an airplane, flying up into the air. Notice also that 士 *shì* is like an inverted 干 *gān (See Chapter 2).*

工 gōng work; labour

工 *gōng* was a picture of a very handy tool for craftsmen, which was kind of like a double-headed hammer. For that reason, it became the character for "work." To an English speaker, it most resembles a capital letter I, but with longer horizontal lines. 工 *gōng* is commonly used in 工作 gōng zuò, the word for "job."

工 *gōng*, 士 *shì*, 土 *tǔ* all look similar, so it's important to keep in mind the little differences that distinguish them.

力 lì strength, power

力 *lì* was a tool for breaking up soil in the field. To do this kind of work, you need strength, and so that is the meaning of this character. Think of the longest downstroke as a person's body, and the horizontal stroke as his outstretched arm. The smaller downstroke is the farm tool that this character is based on, and he is hard at work, ploughing the field.

Alternatively, you can think of the whole character as the bottom of this tool, ready to dig into the ground.

功 gōng merit, achievement, effect, success.

功 *gōng* is a combination of 工 *gōng* and 力 *lì*. (Notice that 功 gōng and 工 gōng are pronounced exactly the same, even though they are different characters.) Since this character is a combination of "work" and "strength," it means "achievement" or "success," because if you have ability and you work hard, you will achieve your goals.

You have probably heard of Kung Fu, which is the old spelling of 功夫 *gōng fū*. If you remember from Chapter 1, 夫 *fū* means an adult male. Putting the two words together, we see that although 功夫 *gōng fū* has become the name for Chinese martial arts, its actual meaning is "a man of great skill and achievement."

Anyone who works hard, putting in time and effort towards a goal, can be said to have 功夫 *gōng fū*. If you work hard at learning Chinese, you will make steady progress, and one day you, too, can be said to have 功夫 *gōng fū!*

Practice.

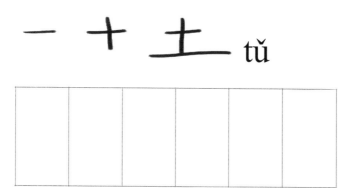 tǔ

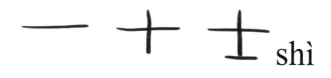

 shì

一 丅 工

gōng

フカ lì

エ エカ gōng

105

Chapter 11

太 **tài** too much / big, used in front of

adjectives.

太 tài is composed of a 大 dà and a dot. We know that 大 dà means big (Chapter 1), so we can think of 太 tài in this way: 大 dà is big enough, add a little more (a dot), and then it is too big, as in 太大 tài dà - "Too big!"

The original character from the Xiǎo zhuàn style reminds me of a man wearing some kind of shackles around his ankles, as though he were a prisoner - "too much" for society. But this isn't as clear in the current form of the character.

A funny thing I would like to share with you: One title for a wife or married woman is 太太 tàitai. Does this mean that a wife can be just too much to bear?

犬 quǎn dog

We can see from the way that 犬 quǎn has changed that it has nothing to do with "big." It is a word for "dog." The ancient character does look like a dog. Then the Xiǎo zhuàn character changes to look more like a man shooting a bow and arrow. The current character doesn't look anything like a dog, so I like to think of it as a man holding a ball that he is about to throw to his dog. Go fetch!

头 tóu head

The Xiǎo zhuàn tǐ of 头 tóu is very complicated. Its left half is a big round container, as we can see above, while the right half is a word for "brain" or the beginning part of something, so together they mean a brain container, which of course is our head.

The current character, fortunately, is a lot simpler than the ancient version. It is 大 dà with two dots on the upper left. I think of the dots as some kind of energy coming out of the man's head. Maybe he's having an idea. Or maybe he has a throbbing headache - 头疼 tóu téng.

头 tóu, 犬 quǎn, and 太 dài are all based on 大 dà, but with the dots in different places. A dot under 大 dà is too much. A dot

109

up on the right is something always barks but put its head behind. In Chinese, another more common word for "dog" - 狗 gǒu - is also often used in phrases that are vulgar or insulting. English has something similar, but I'm not going to spell it out here. You can guess it for yourself!

Two dots up on the left also means somebody walks in front of others and has intelligence. In Chinese culture, left is the front or higher position, right is behind or the lower position. This is why the Chinese have always considered being left-handed as good luck and a sign of being clever, whereas in the West, it was considered as some kind of problem or defect.

We will look at some more characters based on 大 dà, but these are a bit more complicated.

哭 kū cry

哭 kū is a word that has a picture in it: two big eyes written as 口 kǒu (Chapter 5), a teardrop, and a 大 dà. I like to think of it as a face, with a tear coming out of one eye and a running nose.

笑 xiào laugh

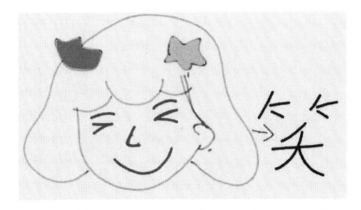

In 笑 xiào, we see almost the same face as in 哭 kū, but here, the eyes are closed because the person is laughing. Notice also that there are two horizontal lines instead of one. (You might think this looks like 天 tiān from Chapter 1, but it's actually a different character, 夭 yǎo. The difference is the slight slant of the top line.) When we laugh or smile, our face has more wrinkles, and so you can think of the extra line in this way. I read a news story about a model who wouldn't allow herself to ever smile or laugh because she didn't want to get wrinkles. This story made me laugh, because I guess she doesn't know that faces are most beautiful when they are smiling.

器 qì　instrument, piece of equipment

器 qì is made of 犬 quǎn and four 口 kǒu. But these four 口 kǒu don't mean mouths, they are containers. 器 qì is a picture of a dog and four containers. In the old days, this might be what a hunter would take with him when he went out to hunt. The containers hold his equipment, and that is what this character means.

器 qì is often used in combination words to designate specific types of equipment. For example, 武器 wǔqì is the word for weapons, or military equipment, and 乐器 yuèqì is the word for musical instrument.

Practice.

一 ナ 大 太 tài

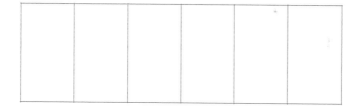

一 ナ 大 犬 quǎn

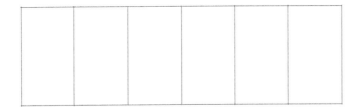

tóu

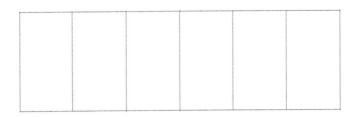

kū

116

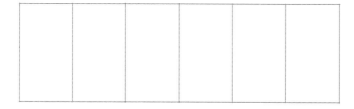 xiào

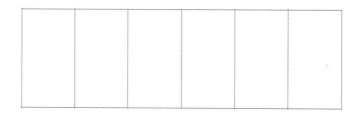 qì

Chapter 12

<u>上</u> shàng

up; above; indicating that an action has started. Two commonly used phrases:上车shàng chē — get on the vehicle; 上课 shàng kè — having a class.

下 xià

down; below; indicating the finalizing of an action. Two commonly used phrases:下车xià chē — get off the vehicle; 下课 xià kè — class is over.

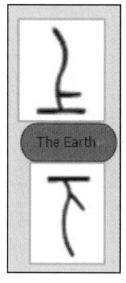
The Earth

When the ancients first invented the characters, I think that coming up with characters for things we can see was probably not too difficult. But making a picture of something we can't see, like our thoughts, or directions, is really something difficult.

I think when my ancestors tried to describe 上 shàng and 下 xià, they put the character 一 yī in these two words as an image of the ground. 上 shàng is something growing up from the Earth. You can think of it as a plant, with a main stem and one branch coming off the side. Plants naturally grow upwards towards the sun.

119

This image also works for 下 xià, because plants don't only have stems, they also have roots, which grown down into the ground to absorb water and nutrients.

上 shàng and 下 xià can be a little confusing for Westerners, because they don't look like the Up and Down arrows that are used in Western culture. In fact, they almost look like the opposite — 上 shàng looks more like a down arrow, and 下 xià looks more like an up arrow. This is why it's important to remember that in both characters, the horizontal stroke symbolizes the earth, and the other strokes are either growing up from it, or down into it.

卡 qiǎ to block, get stuck, be

jammed

kǎ block, check, card

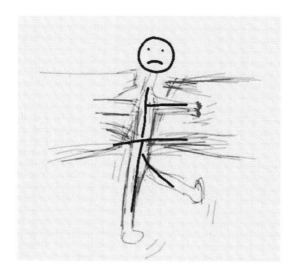

So what happens when an unstoppable force meets an immovable object? The same thing that happens when you try to go up and down at the same time - gridlock!

You can see that 卡 qiǎ has 上 shàng and 下 xià together as one character. Up and down cancel each other out, and so this word means to get stuck or blocked.

This character is also used to mean "card," like a credit card or membership card. When used this way, it is pronounced kǎ. This is easy to remember because of the phonetic similarity between "card" and kǎ, although the character itself doesn't really hint at this meaning. This kind of transliteration also appears in 卡路里 kǎlùli — calorie, 卡丁车 kǎdīngchē — carting car, and 卡通 kǎtōng — cartoon.

小 xiǎo   small, little

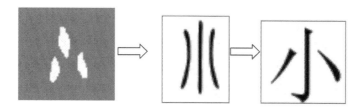

小 xiǎo was a character for 少 shǎo (a little; less) and 沙 shā (sand), and it meant "sand" or "little rocks." But after people made 少 shǎo and 沙 shā, the meaning of 小 xiǎo changed to "small." Though it's difficult to see this meaning in the shape of the character today, you can see it clearly in the old Xiǎo zhuàn version, which shows three little grains of sand.

Remember that 大 dà is the character for "big," and is based on the character for a person. If you compare 大 dà and 小 xiǎo, you can think of 大 dà as a big man standing with his legs spread apart and his arms sticking out. In contrast, 小 xiǎo is like a little child — 小孩子 xiǎoháizi — standing with his legs together and his arms angled down at his sides. And you can use 大 dà and 小 xiǎo this way: 大人 dà ren — adults, 小孩 xiǎohái — little kids.

小 xiǎo is a very simple character, and a very common one, and so you will learn it just by seeing it over and over again in many different words and sentences.

尖 jiān point; tip; top; pointed

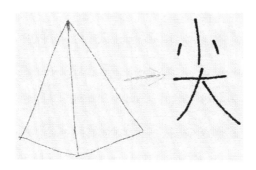

Speaking of 小 xiǎo and 大 dà together, our next character is 尖 jiān, which is composed of both a 小 xiǎo and a 大 dà in order to symbolize something that is big on one end and small on the other, like a pyramid or an arrowhead. Pyramids and arrows are pointed, and that is the meaning of 尖 jiān.

尖 jiān and 卡 qiǎ are both characters in which two words are joined together to make one word, (like compound words in English) and convey the meaning in a very clear and funny way — if you know the meaning of the two characters being combined! In Chinese, there are a lot of words like this.

Practice.

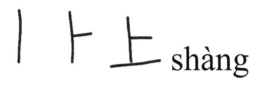 shàng

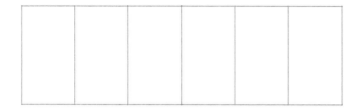

 xià

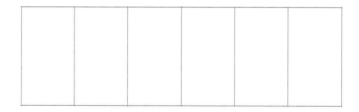

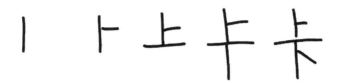

qiǎ; kǎ

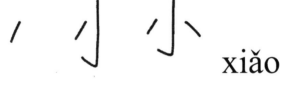

xiǎo

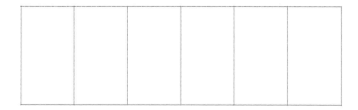

jiān

Chapter 13

門 mén door; gate

You can see that the earlier vision of 門 mén — which is still used in Hong Kong, Taiwan, and some other places — looks more like a picture of a doorway than the current version. Actually, the earlier version looks like two swinging doors, like saloon doors in the old west. Doors in ancient China were similar to this, which is why the old character looks this way.

The current version is still easy to remember, because you can see that it looks like an enclosed area, with a small opening in the upper left corner. You can think of the little dot as the door that lets you in to the walled off area.

问 wèn ask; inquire

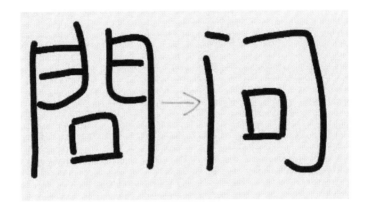

问 wèn means to ask. It is a picture of a mouth — 口 kǒu — inside a room with a door. The original meaning was a man locked in a room being interrogated by policemen. Nowadays it just means to ask or inquire. I guess society has become a little more polite.

间 **jiān** time; among or between; room

间 **jiàn** within a definite time or space

You remember that we learned 日 rì, the character for the sun, in Chapter 7. Here, we have a picture of the sun inside a door. The original meaning of 间 jiān was that the sunlight goes through the door, and so people can tell the time by the angle or shadow on the ground. Before human beings invented mechanical clocks, they had sundials to tell time.

间 jiān is used in many different combination words, and can have several different meanings. For example, 时间 shí jiān refers to the concept of time, and 空间 kōng jiān refers to the concept of space.

间 jiān has two different pronunciations — one with the first tone, and another with the fourth. It's an important character that is used in many different words.

Practice.

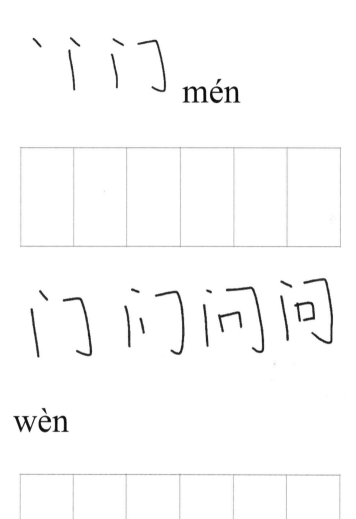

`丶 讠 讠 门` mén

`门 门 讠 讠 问 问 问` wèn

jiān; jiàn

Chapter 14

白 bái white

In the old days, 白 bái meant "bright," because it is a picture of a burning candle. Later, people began using 明 míng for bright, (we'll talk about 明 míng later in this chapter) and so 白 bái took on a new meaning: white.

You can see that 白 bái is the character for the sun, 日 rì, with an extra dot on top. Although the sun is often shown as yellow in paintings and drawings, the light of the sun is actually white. You can think of the extra dot as a ray of sunlight to help you remember this character.

百 bǎi   hundred

If we add a horizontal line (一 yī) to the top of 白 bái, then we have a new character with a different pronunciation. 百 bǎi means "hundred," and is pronounced with the third tone, not like 白 bái which is the second tone. These two tones are often the hardest for students of Chinese to differentiate, but with practice, you will get it!

There isn't really anything in the picture of 百 bǎi to make you think of the number one hundred, so you'll just have to remember that 一 yī plus 白 bái equals the character for "hundred." As a count word for a very common number, this is a character that you will encounter many times. 一百 yī bǎi, one hundred, 二百 èr bǎi, two hundred, and so on.

皇 huáng emperor, king

In Chapter 7, we learned that 王 wáng means "king." Here, we have the character for king with the character for "white" above it. Remember that 白 bái is based on the character for "sun," and so 皇 huáng is a picture of the king and the sun together.

Many ancient cultures, including the Romans and also the Chinese, associated kings and emperors with the sun, because the sun was seen as the supreme ruler of heaven.

In the ancient Xiǎo zhuàn version of the character, it looks like the king character has a crown on his head. So you can think of 白 bái as the emperor's crown. If you're a fan of the Beatles, just think of that song "Sun King" from Abbey Road!

月 yuè the moon

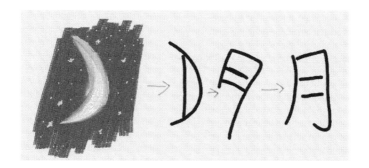

月 yuè, the character for the moon, has changed a lot from its early shape. Now it looks like 目 mù — the character for "eye" — without the third line at the bottom, or like 日 rì Chapter 7) with a longer, open bottom.

Remember that 日 rì is the character for the sun. 月 yuè is open at the bottom because the moon gets its light from the sun, so it needs to have an opening to absorb the energy from the sun.

月 yuè and 肉 ròu - the character for "flesh" - are not connected, but nonetheless, lots of words in Chinese have 月 yuè as a radical to signify a body part. In the next section, we'll see why.

肉 ròu meat

Look at the old Xiǎo zhuàn versions of 月 yuè and 肉 ròu — you can see that they started with almost the same shape. In order to not confuse them, now they are different. But when 肉 ròu is used as a radical, it looks like its old shape, which we write like 月 yuè.

This character 肉 ròu has two 人 rén in it (Book 1, Chapter 1). To me, it looks like one guy is doing pull-ups on a bar, while the other guy is on the ground, cheering him on. "加油 Jiā Yóu! 加油 Jiā Yóu!" *

We do pull-ups or other exercises to build muscle, which is meat, so you can remember the meaning of the character that way.

* 加油 jiā yóu means something like "C'mon!" or "Go! Go!" The literal meaning, though, is "add oil."

夕 **xī** evening

月 yuè and 夕 xī also started out as the same shape. In the Xiǎo zhuàn characters, people added one more dot for 月 yuè. 夕 xī keep the angle of the early shape, whereas 月 yuè became vertical.

夕 xī is usually used in "夕阳 xī yáng," which means the evening sun — sunset.

明 míng bright; clear

We learned that the original meaning of 白 bái is "bright," but that it later changed to the color white. So people made 明 míng for "bright." I like this character because it has the sun and the moon together — it must be the brightest thing in the world!

明 míng is used with 白 bái to make 明白 míng bái which means "clear" and also "understand." If someone is telling you something, and you want to tell them that you've got it, you say, "明白 míng bái."

We use the English word "clear" in the same way, as in "Do I make myself clear?"

Does this character remind you of the word 晶 jīng in Chapter 7? Remember, three 日 rì makes 晶 jīng.

Practice.

 bái

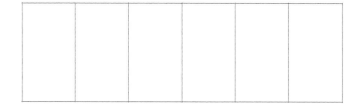 bǎi

白 白 白 皀 皁 皇 huáng

丿 几 月 月 yuè

丨 冂 内 肉 ròu

ノ ク 夕 xī

151

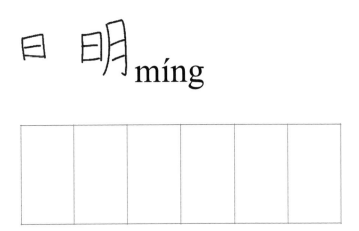
日 明 míng

Thank you for reading the whole book. Hope you enjoyed it! Now we can do some guessing and learning! Through this exercise, you will know more about how Chinese phrases are made.

Guessing practice. Match the Chinese phrases to the English meanings

Round 1

1. 十平米 shí píng mǐ ＿＿

2. 森林 sēn lín ＿＿

3. 未来 wèi lái ＿＿

4. 回来 huí lái ＿＿

5. 水火不容 shuǐ huǒ bù róng ＿＿

A. come back

B. ten square meter

C. forest

D. future

E. oil and water don't mix

Round 2

1. 日出 rì chū   ___

2. 早上好 zǎo shàng hǎo ___

3. 儿女 ér nǚ   ___

4. 光明 guāng míng   ___

5. 停止 tíng zhǐ   ___

A. good morning

B. bright

C. stop

D. daughter and son

E. sunrise

Round 3

1. 兄弟 xiōng dì   ___

2. 舌头 shé tou   ___

3. 说话 shuō huà   ___

4. 士兵 shì bīng   ___

5. 工作 gōng zuò   ___

A. work/job

B. brothers/dude

C. talk/chat

D. tongue

E. soldier

Round 4

1. 功夫gōng fu   ___

2. 土地tǔ dì   ___

3. 太大tàidà   ___

4. 头发tóu fa   ___

5. 哭泣kū qì   ___

A. cry

B. land

C. Kong Fu

D. too big

E. hair

Round 5

1. 微笑wēi xiào   ___

2. 尖利jiān lì   ___

3. 卡片kǎ piàn   ___

4. 卡通kǎ tōng   ___

5. 大门dà mén   ___

A. gate

B. smile

C. cartoon

D. sharp/pointy

E. card

Round 6

1. 问题wèn tí   ___

2. 明白míng bai   ___

3. 白色bái sè   ___

4. 太阳tài yáng   ___

5. 阳光yáng guāng ___

A. sunshine

B. sun

C. understand/ clear

D. white

E. question/problem

159

Round 7

1. 上车 shàng chē   ___

2. 下楼 xià lóu   ___

3. 月亮 yuè liang   ___

4. 月光 yuè guāng   ___

5. 一百 yī bǎi   ___

A. go down the stairs

B. The moon

C. moonlight

D. one hundred

E. board the vehicle

Round 8

1. 夕阳xī yáng   ____

2. 牛肉niú ròu   ____

3. 两百元liǎng bǎi yuán ____

4. 白头发bái tóu fà   ____

5. 小水晶xiǎo shuǐ jīng ____

A. beef

B. two hundred RMB

C. sunset

D. white hair

E. little crystal

Answers to the Guessing practice.

Round 1   1. B 2. C 3. D 4. A 5. E

Round 2   1. E 2. A 3. D 4. B 5. C

Round 3   1. B 2. D 3. C 4. E 5. A

Round 4   1. C 2. B 3. D 4. E 5. A

Round 5   1. B 2. D 3. E 4. C 5. A

Round 6   1. E 2. C 3. D 4. B 5. A

Round 7   1. E 2. A 3. B 4. C 5. D

Round 8   1. C 2. A 3. B 4. D 5. E

Look out for the next book! Since we learned a lot of basic parts, we can start to having fun mixing parts to learn more new characters!

Printed in Great Britain
by Amazon